# NEW ORLEANS-STYLE COOKING

### Kate Cranshaw

# NEW ORLEANS-STYLE COOKING

## Kate Cranshaw

COURAGE
BOOKS

AN IMPRINT OF RUNNING PRESS
PHILADELPHIA · LONDON

*Previous page: an 1889 illustration of a restaurant in the French quarter of New Orleans. Right: a caricature of a couple in a New Orleans restaurant trying to placate a vagrant with a glass of wine.*

CLB 4171
9 8 7 6 5 4 3 2 1
Digit on the right indicates the number of this
printing.

Library of Congress Cataloging-in-Publication
Number 93-87602

ISBN 1-56138-446-1

This book was designed and produced by
CLB Publishing, Godalming, Surrey, England.

Editor: Kate Cranshaw
Senior Editor: Jillian Stewart
Introduction: Bill Harris
Designers: Stonecastle Graphics
Picture Researcher: Leora Kahn
Photographers: Neil Sutherland and Peter Barry

Typesetting by Inforum
Printed and bound in Singapore

Published by Courage Books,
an imprint of Running Press Book Publishers
125 South Twenty-second Street
Philadelphia, PA 19103-4399

# Contents

# Introduction

*Above: an 1872 steel engraving of New Orleans' busy port.*

There are all kinds of ways to have fun in New Orleans, but when all is said and done, it is the food that makes the Crescent City so much more fun than any other city in the world. Most regional cuisines usually revolve around one or two specialties, but in New Orleans it includes everything from soup to nuts, or, more accurately, from crawfish bisque to pralines, with something special every step of the way between the Ramos gin fizz that precedes a typical New Orleans meal and the chicory-laced coffee that tops it off.

Jazz music is generally considered the city's greatest gift to the world, but one of its greatest interpreters, Louis Armstrong, always signed his

*Right: a quiet day on Madison Street, New Orleans.*

letters "Red beans and ricely yours ..." not only as a way of remembering his roots but to remind his friends that food is also one his native city's great gifts to the pleasures of life. And at the same time he was giving a new meaning to one of the tunes he made famous, "Do You Know What it Means to Miss New Orleans?"

To miss New Orleans is to miss a whole lot more than red beans and rice. It means nostalgia for crawfish pie and Louisiana gumbo, jambalaya and dirty rice, shrimp Creole and Cajun pies, pralines and bread pudding and so much more. But if it has been a while since you have had the pleasure of visiting Café du Monde in Jackson Square for some hot, feathery light beignets or enjoyed a romantic Creole dinner in the courtyard at Brennan's, you can recapture some of the flavors you miss through the recipes in the following pages. And if you have never been lucky enough to visit New Orleans you will soon get a taste for it.

One of New Orleans' most popular and famous ingredients, not only in local kitchens, but around the world, is the liquid form of cayenne pepper called Tabasco. The McIlhenny Company, the world's only manufacturer of bottled Tabasco, sells more than 10 million bottles of it every year; and every one of them carries a little bit of New Orleans along with it.

This wonderful elixir was developed a little over a century ago when red pepper seeds were imported from Mexico and planted on Avery Island, a little spit of land that rises 150 feet above the swamps and bayous about 125 miles west of New Orleans. The pepper plants thrived there and took on a character

*Above: an old Spanish-tiled building typical of many in turn-of-the-century New Orleans.*

of their own thanks, in part, to the fact that Avery's base is a block of pure salt. And if the salt helps makes the cayenne a little more peppery, it is also one of the reasons why all the bottled Tabasco in the world is made right there on Avery Island.

The process begins in the fall when the reddest of the peppers are picked by hand. Then the freshly-harvested crop is covered with salt and mashed to a pulp. The mash is placed in oak barrels, covered with more salt and then capped with a perforated lid designed to keep the air out but to allow the gasses caused by fermentation to escape. The fermenting process lasts a full three years and when the barrels are finally opened, vinegar is added and the mixture is churned for a month. After that, it is strained, filtered and bottled, ready to add a dash of zest to just about anything you happen to be cooking.

Almost anything from a New Orleans kitchen makes a meal a fun-filled adventure. But in spite of the famous WPA Guide published in the 1930s, which cautioned its readers, "If you have no faith in the potency of herbs and seasonings, don't try Creole cooking," not everything is spicy and pungent. Variety is the real spice of the New Orleans style. Lousiana cuisine, like so many other American styles of cooking, is a combination of influences refined over generations into something quite different from any of its original ingredients.

One of the most obvious influences is French. When the first settlers arrived at the mouth of the Mississippi River from France back at the end of the 17th century, they brought their culinary skills along with them, but they were forced to improvise and adapt their original recipes to new and strange ingredients.

The language of New Orleans cuisine is as unique as its flavors. Jambalaya, for instance, has its roots in the Spanish paella, but the name probably comes from the French word "jambon," meaning ham, and the African word "ya," which means rice, to which the French-speaking local cooks added their own favorite culinary description, "à la." But if the original was a rice dish cooked with ham, it is just as commonly made with beef and pork and sausage as well as ham and shellfish, quite frequently all together. Gumbo is another classic dish of which the name itself is a clue to some of the influences that were at work in its origin. It comes from the African word, "gombo," for a vegetable introduced to the Americas by the slave

*Above: the intriguing architecture of a New Orleans' courtyard.*

trade. We call it okra, and it is one of the two basic thickening agents in nearly all gumbos. The other is filé, a powder made by grinding dried sassafras leaves, that was widely used by the Choctaw Indians in their cooking for generations before the first settlers arrived. Later rice and other spices were added to the basic recipe, but even today, this unique dish is as fascinatingly varied as a New Orleans street scene. Once the basics have been established – a good roux, some okra or filé and a pile of fresh vegetables – the rest is a combination of whatever is on hand.

Cajuns generally consider filé gumbo made with chicken or sausages or even squirrel and armadillo to be the most authentic version of this New Orleans classic, but many Cajun cooks also often add fresh oysters to their tasty meat dish just before serving. Among the Creoles of New Orleans, the traditional gumbo is almost invariably made with seafood, including hardshell crabs and local shrimp, and okra. Which version is the real thing? Probably neither, but considering the creative possibilities, sticking with the original wouldn't be nearly as much fun.

Any extra additions might be called a *lagniappe*, a word common in New Orleans to describe a little something extra. Although its original meaning is about the same as the tip you leave behind for a waiter, it is frequently used in Louisiana cooking, too, to describe those little surprises the recipe didn't specify but that have allowed the cook to make a personal statement. Lagniappes are common possibly because most of the original recipes are based on oral tradition. Even when the first local cookbooks began appearing about a hundred years ago, they left just about everything to the imagination. A typical entry in one of them was to "Take a nice fish, season to taste, cook until done and serve."

Even when recipes are more specific, the language differences in those old cookbooks are forever confounding strangers – those tasty little crustaceans that are called crayfish the world over are crawfish in New Orleans. It is the same creature, but watch the spelling when you visit the Crescent City or you'll be marked as a tourist. On the other hand, what better reason can there be to make a visit? But time the trip carefully. The crawfish season begins in November and reaches its peak in May and June before ending completely in July. Some restaurants that specialize in crawfish dishes simply close their doors for the other four months; others sadly change their menus.

Oysters, it is said, should only be eaten in months with "R" in their spelling, but in New Orleans where oysters are the staff of life, they are a year 'round treat in dozens of different ways; from freshly-shucked on the half-shell at backyard picnics, to such gloriously elegant dishes as oysters rockefeller. This classic New Orleans creation has its culinary roots in escargots bourgignons, another French delicacy. Although the early French settlers couldn't find the right kind of snails to suit their taste, oysters seemed to be a perfect substitute and the combination of salt water from the Gulf of Mexico mingled with the fresh water of local lakes and rivers made them not only unusually abundant, but arguably the best-tasting in the world.

The subtropical climate of southern Louisiana produces an incredible variety and abundance of fresh fruits and vegetables, too, and all of it has found its way into the tradition of New Orleans cooking. No matter where they came from, the original Creoles used what they found locally to match the cooking styles they left behind. Cajuns, too, adapted an old cuisine to the bounty of the New World, but if there is a difference today between Creole and Cajun cooking, it might be said that the latter is closer to the cuisine of southern France (but don't say that above a whisper in Bordeaux).

The reason is that the Cajun people themselves are so close to their own roots in France, even though the first of them arrived in Louisiana in 1765 and they came from Canada, not France. They were French farmers who had originally migrated to Nova Scotia, which they called Acadia, but were driven into exile when the British took over and they refused to switch their loyalties, abandon their Catholic religion or give up their language. In the diaspora, families were broken apart and the Acadians seemed doomed to eternal wandering in search of lost loved ones. Many of them drifted back to France, but several shiploads of them wound up in New Orleans. It would be pleasant to report that, like other immigrant groups, they assimilated into the mosaic, but the fact is they didn't like New Orleans, which was a Spanish colony at the time. They liked the idea that so many of the people who greeted them at the levee spoke their language, but they would have been just as discontented if the city had been Paris itself. The Acadian wanderers were farmers; and cities simply made them uncomfortable.

They were quite comfortable in the rich, fertile land of southwest Louisiana, though, and they created new communities of their own along Bayou Teche and Bayou Lafourche, where they lived in relative isolation, keeping their culture alive and, probably most important of all, adapting their culinary style to the produce of the New Eden. Other Acadians joined them, and by 1785, there were half-a-million of them living out in the bayous, raising livestock and planting sweet potatoes and sugar cane. When Napoleon repossessed Louisana in 1800, nothing changed in the lives of the Acadians, and when he sold it to the Americans three years later, life in the bayous went on as it had been with no thought of change. Many of the Acadians had built substantial plantations by then, and the 36-mile strip of the Mississippi separating St. James and Ascension parishes, the heart of Cajun Country, was already known as Louisiana's "Golden Coast." Still, the majority continued living as they had up in Acadia, tending little farms as "petits habitants," small landholders.

They had an old mistrust of education and most

*Above: an 1883 engraving of New Orleans' cotton levee depicting the busy daily activity of traders.*

Acadian children learned the basics of farming and domestic skills at home; where they were usually part of extended families that included aunts, uncles and grandparents as well as their own parents. Entire families worked together on the farms and made group efforts of hunting and fishing. Over the years, although the world around them was changing, the Acadians themselves didn't change a thing about their lifestyle. And what changed least of all was the daily routine in their kitchens.

Change finally came to the bayous after World War I, when new roads and bridges began to end the isolation of Cajun Country. Farming became mechanized and more efficient, and radio and the movies began altering the ideas of the young. When the state made education compulsory, youngsters were not only forced to go to school, but found their language outlawed there. Even when the law was changed in the 1940s and foreign languages became part of the curriculum, modern French was the language taught, and not Cajun, which was the same as the language spoken in France in the 17th century. In more recent times, the discovery of oil and gas in the Gulf of Mexico has brought strangers into their midst, and the Cajun way of life has changed even more. But fortunately for the rest of us, the Acadian culinary tradition has hardly been altered since the first of them arrived in Lousiana more than two hundred years ago. And even better news is that, thanks to such chefs as Paul Prudhomme, such Cajun classics as blackened redfish and crawfish étouffée have recently become as classically American as apple pie.

Most New Orleans cuisine has been known for generations as Creole cooking. The word "Creole" itself has dozens of meanings. In its original form, it comes from the Portuguese colonists in Brazil who were among the first to bring slaves into the Americas. In the American South, the word "Creole" was used to distinguish a native-born slave from one who had recently arrived from Africa. The word took on yet another meaning after the Louisiana Purchase in 1803, when New Orleanians of French and Spanish descent began calling themselves Creoles as a way of setting themselves apart from the Americans who were beginning to arrive in huge numbers. Their city had existed for more than a century and although it shared the same continent as the United States, most of these new self-styled Creoles believed that the similarity ended there, and that they were about to be invaded by Barbarians. For their part, the puritanical Americans thought the Creoles were a decadent lot and generally regarded it as a blessing when they were snubbed by their new neighbors.

The result was a standoff. The Americans responded to the hostility by building a city of their own separated from the Creole districts by the city moat, which has given Canal Street its name, and each segment of society went its own way, pretending that the other didn't exist. As the Americans grew richer, the Creoles grew poorer and in the interest of family pride, the old New Orleans establishment began encouraging its sons and daughters to intermarry with the newcomers. It gave their cooks a new influence to contend with, but they had assimilated new ideas before and they were quite up to the challenge. The climate and the available local produce were still at the bottom of it all, and these Americans were as enchanted by the food of New Orleans as with the city itself.

All the barriers between Creole and American came crashing down when American soldiers and sailors arrived to defend the Crescent City against British invaders at the end of the War of 1812. Far more than the Louisiana Purchase, it confirmed once and for all that New Orleans was an American city. But even now, after all these years, it is an American city with a difference. And the biggest difference of all is in the food, which is always the single most satisfying experience New Orleans has to offer.

The word that sums it all up is tradition. The 1930s guidebook prepared by the Federal Writer's Project described it perfectly, and the words are as true in the 1990s as they were 60 years ago:

"Although the Creoles are lavish entertainers and can prepare a sumptuous meal which is the source of never-ending pleasure to the gourmet," the Guide noted, "they also follow the French trait of economy and were taught early in life the secret of a perfect blending of a quantity of well-cooked simple foods which are nourishing, but not a strain on the budget."

In those days, according to the book (in one of the great understatements of the entire series), "Native Orleanians are fond of seafood and will drive miles to partake of any well-seasoned dish of this delicacy." Where most of them went back in those days was to the shores of Lake Pontchartrain, where food stands served free oysters, crabs, shrimp, and crayfish to anyone who bought a glass of beer. The days of the free lunch are long gone, but in those days southern Louisiana was the only place to enjoy Creole and Cajun specialties at any price. In our time, the basic ingredients are available nearly everywhere; just waiting to be lovingly assembled into a feast that celebrates the unique style of this city. Sure, they still have big fun down by the bayou, but as you are about to discover for yourself, there is almost as much fun to be had in your own kitchen and dining room as anywhere in the New Orleans area.

*Above: the old French Opera House on Bourbon Street.*

# CHAPTER ONE

# Soups and Appetizers

*Above: traders selling their wares amid the hub of activity on the levee.*

Cajun and Creole soups tend to be thick and hearty often like a stew, but the most well known and the most refined is the Bisque. Usually based on crawfish, crab, or shrimp and traditionally garnished with stuffed crawfish heads, this soup is considered a test of skill for any accomplished New Orleans cook as it requires long and complex preparation. Shellfish are often served as an appetizer in New Orleans and other favorite recipes include Oysters Rockefeller, Buster Crabs (tiny soft-shell crabs), and Remoulade.

# Shrimp Bisque

*This classic Cajun recipe owes its origin to the French settlers. Producing a first class bisque is considered a good test for a skilled Louisiana cook, as many recipes are long and complex. This recipe is a simplified version.*

*3 Tbsps butter or margarine*
*1 onion, finely chopped*
*1 red bell pepper, finely chopped*
*2 stalks celery, finely chopped*
*1 clove garlic, minced*
*Pinch dry mustard and cayenne pepper*
*2 tsps paprika*
*3 Tbsps flour*
*4 cups fish stock*
*1 sprig thyme and a bay leaf*
*8 oz raw, peeled shrimp*
*Salt and pepper*
*Snipped chives*

*Melt the butter or margarine in a saucepan. Add the onion, bell pepper, celery, and garlic. Cook gently to soften. Stir in the mustard, cayenne, paprika, and flour. Cook about 3 minutes over gentle heat, stirring occasionally. Pour on the stock gradually, stirring until well blended. Add the thyme and bay leaf and bring to a boil. Reduce the heat and simmer about 5 minutes or until thickened, stirring occasionally. Add the shrimp and cook gently until pink and curled – about 5 minutes. Season with salt and pepper to taste, remove the bay leaf and top with snipped chives before serving.*
*Serves 6.*

## Gumbo z'Herbes

*Gumbo is an African contribution to Louisiana cooking.*

*8 oz green cabbage leaves*
*8 oz spinach, well washed*
*1 pound spring greens, collard, mustard, beet or turnip greens*
*4 oz Belgian endive*
*1 large bunch watercress, well washed*
*1 large bunch parsley, well washed*
*6 carrot and radish tops (if available)*
*4 cups water*
*2 Tbsps butter or margarine*
*1 large red bell pepper, coarsely chopped*
*½ bunch green onions, coarsely chopped*
*8 oz okra, trimmed and sliced*
*1 bay leaf*
*1 tsp thyme*
*Salt, pepper, and a pinch cayenne*
*Pinch cinnamon and nutmeg*

*Trim any coarse stalks on the cabbage and spinach and wash both well. Wash greens, Belgian endive, watercress, parsley, and carrot and radish tops. Bring the water to a boil in a large stock pot and add the greens, spinach, cabbage, Belgian endive, watercress, and parsley, and carrot and radish tops. Return to a boil, reduce heat and simmer, partially covered, for about 2 hours. Strain and reserve the liquid. Purée the vegetables in a food processor until smooth, and return to the rinsed out pot. Measure the liquid and make up to 3 cups with water, if necessary. Melt the butter or margarine in a pan, add the bell pepper, onions, and okra. Cook briefly and add to the gumbo. Add the bay leaf, thyme, seasoning, and spices and cook another 30 minutes over gentle heat. Remove the bay leaf, adjust the seasoning and serve. Serves 6.*

# Red Bean and Red Pepper Soup

## Chicken and Shrimp Peppers

*The French and Spanish influences on Creole cooking are very evident in the common usage of bell peppers in recipes.*

3 large green or red bell peppers
¼ cup butter or margarine
1 small onion, finely chopped
1 stalk celery, finely chopped
1 clove garlic, minced
2 chicken breasts, skinned, boned and finely diced
4 oz cooked, peeled shrimp
2 tsps chopped parsley
Salt, pepper, and a pinch cayenne pepper
½ loaf of stale French bread, made into crumbs
1-2 eggs, beaten
6 tsps dry bread crumbs

*Beans have been used as a cheap and nutritious filler in New Orleans cooking for many generations, and they are as popular today as they have ever been.*

1 pound dried red kidney beans
Water, to cover
2 onions, coarsely chopped
3 stalks celery, coarsely chopped
2 bay leaves
Salt and pepper
3 large red bell peppers, finely chopped
4 Tbsps red wine
10 cups chicken stock
4 chopped hard-boiled eggs and lemon wedges, to garnish

*Soak the beans in the water overnight. Alternatively, bring them to a boil, boil rapidly for 2 minutes, then leave to stand for 1 hour. Drain off the liquid and add the onions, celery, bay leaves, salt and pepper, bell peppers, red wine, and stock. Bring to a boil over high heat, stirring occasionally. Reduce heat and simmer, partially covered, for about 3 hours, or until the beans are completely tender. Remove bay leaves and purée the soup in a food processor or blender. Serve garnished with the chopped hard-boiled eggs. Serve lemon wedges on the side. Serves 8-10.*

*Cut the bell peppers in half lengthwise and remove the cores and seeds. Leave the stems attached, if desired. Melt the butter in a skillet and add the onion, celery, garlic, and chicken. Cook over moderate heat until the vegetables are softened and the chicken is cooked. Add the shrimp and parsley. Season with salt, pepper, and cayenne. Stir in the French bread crumbs and add enough beaten egg to make the mixture hold together. Spoon filling into each bell pepper half, mounding the top slightly, and place in a baking dish just big enough to hold them. Pour enough water down the inside of the dish to come about ½ inch up the sides of the peppers. Cover and bake in a pre-heated 350° F oven for about 45 minutes, or until the peppers are just tender. Sprinkle each with the dried bread crumbs and place under a preheated broiler until golden brown. Serve hot or cold. Serves 6.*

# Chicken and Sausage Jambalaya

*Jambalaya is a hearty one-pot dish which can be made with whatever ingredients you have to hand. Ham is a popular addition, which may be linked to its name as the first part relates to both the French and Spanish words for ham. Served as a main course it will feed 4-6.*

*3 pounds chicken portions, skinned, boned, and cut into cubes (bones and skin reserved)*
*1 large onion, roughly chopped*
*3 stalks celery, roughly chopped*
*3 Tbsps butter or margarine*
*1 large green bell pepper, roughly chopped*
*1 clove garlic, minced*
*1 tsp each cayenne, white, and black pepper*
*1 cup uncooked rice*
*14 oz canned tomatoes*
*6 oz andouille (smoked pork) sausage cut into ½-inch dice*
*3 cups chicken stock*
*Chopped parsley, to garnish*

*Use the chicken bones and skin, and onion and celery trimmings to make stock. Cover the ingredients with water, bring to a boil and then simmer slowly for 1 hour. Strain and reserve. Melt the butter or margarine in a large saucepan and add the onion. Cook slowly to brown and then add the celery, bell pepper, and garlic; cook briefly. Add the three kinds of pepper and the rice, stirring to mix well. Add the chicken, tomatoes, sausage, and stock. Season and mix well. Bring to a boil, then reduce the heat and simmer about 20-25 minutes, stirring occasionally until the chicken is done and the rice is tender. The rice should have absorbed most of the liquid by the time it has cooked. Garnish with chopped parsley. Serves 8.*

*Above: Hermann-Grima House, on St. Louis Street, was built in 1831 by wealthy merchant Samuel Hermann. The fine exterior is matched by a beautifully decorated and furnished interior.*

# Oysters Rockefeller

*This recipe was invented in 1899 at Antoine's, New Orleans' oldest restaurant. The sauce was said to be as rich as Rockefeller and hence given this name.*

## Crab Meat Balls

*Crab, both soft-shell and hard-shell is a highly regarded shellfish, and appears on menus in many forms. This recipe turns crab meat into a tasty appetizer or snack.*

1 pound fresh or frozen crab meat, chopped finely
4 slices white bread, crusts removed and made into crumbs
1 Tbsp butter or margarine
1 Tbsp flour
½ cup milk
½ red or green chile, seeded and finely chopped
1 green onion, finely chopped
1 Tbsp chopped parsley
Salt
Flour
2 eggs, beaten
Dry bread crumbs
Oil for deep frying

24 oysters, on the half shell
Rock salt
6 strips bacon, finely chopped
1¼ pounds fresh spinach, well washed, stems removed and leaves finely chopped
1 small bunch green onions, finely chopped
2 cloves garlic, minced
4-5 Tbsps fine fresh bread crumbs
Dash of Tabasco
2 Tbsps aniseed liqueur
Pinch salt
Parmesan cheese

*Loosen the oysters from their shells, strain and reserve their liquid. Rinse the shells well and return an oyster to each one. Pour about 1 inch of rock salt into a baking pan and place in the oysters in their shells, pressing each shell gently into the salt. Place the bacon in a large skillet and cook slowly to render it. Turn up the heat and brown the bacon evenly. Add the spinach, green onions, and garlic and cook slowly until softened. Add the bread crumbs, Tabasco, oyster liquid, liqueur, and a pinch of salt. Spoon some of the mixture onto each oyster and sprinkle with Parmesan cheese. Place in a preheated 350° F oven for about 15 minutes. Alternatively, heat through in the oven for 10 minutes and place under a preheated broiler to lightly brown the cheese. Serve immediately. Serves 4.*

*Combine the crab meat with the fresh bread crumbs and set aside. Melt the butter in a pan and add the flour off the heat. Stir in the milk and return to moderate heat. Bring to a boil, stirring constantly. Stir into the crab adding the chile, onion, and parsley. Season to taste, cover and cool completely. Shape the cold mixture into 1-inch balls using floured hands. Coat with beaten egg using a pastry brush, then coat with the dry bread crumbs. Heat oil in a deep sauté pan, or deep-fat fryer to 350° F. Cook for 3 minutes in batches of 6, turning occasionally, or until golden and crisp. Drain on paper towels and sprinkle lightly with salt. Serves 6-8.*

*Above left: Bayou St. John flows towards New Orleans from Lake Pontchartrain. Right: fishermen unload the day's catch onto waiting carts.*

# CHAPTER TWO

# Brunches and Lunches

*Above: begun in the 1790s, the French Market was the place where farmers and other traders sold their goods.*

*In New Orleans the tradition of brunch was started during the late eighteen hundreds, with Bégué's coffee-house in the French quarter cited as the most likely founder. There, "second breakfast" was an extremely lavish affair lasting about an hour and consisting of many courses, both sweet and savory. Today things are not so excessive, but the tradition still thrives, with many of the dishes that were first served over a century ago still making up the main part of the brunch menu in many of New Orleans restaurants. Corn, never far from the heart of any Southerner, is often served for breakfast or brunch, either in the shape of cornbread, cornmeal muffins, or as the Cajun specialty called Coush-Coush. This dish, at its simplest, is merely cornbread soaked in clabber (milk that has soured and turned semisolid in the first stages of making butter).*

# Oeufs Marchand
# de Vin

*Egg dishes make very popular brunch fare. This classic Creole recipe uses not one, but two rich sauces. To make preparation easier, the sauces can be made in advance and then reheated.*

MARCHAND DE VIN SAUCE
*3 Tbsps oil*
*½ small onion, finely chopped*
*1½ Tbsps flour*
*1 clove garlic*
*6 mushrooms, finely chopped*
*¾ cup brown stock*
*6 Tbsps red wine*
*Salt and pepper*

*Full quantity Hollandaise sauce from the recipe for Eggs Sardou (see page 30)*
*4 eggs*
*4 slices smoked bacon*
*4 slices bread*
*Oil for frying*
*1 beefsteak tomato*

*Heat the oil for the Marchand de Vin sauce in a saucepan. Add the onion and cook until softened. Add the flour and cook slowly stirring frequently, until golden brown. Add the garlic and mushrooms and pour on the stock, stirring to blend well. Add the wine and bring the sauce to a boil. Lower the heat and simmer for about 15-20 minutes, stirring occasionally. Season to taste.*

*Prepare the Hollandaise sauce and poach the eggs according to the recipe for Eggs Sardou. Broil the bacon until crisp, then crumble and set aside. Cut the bread with a pastry cutter into 3-inch diameter circles. Fry in enough oil to just cover, until golden brown and crisp. Drain on paper towels and place on a serving plate. Spoon some of the Marchand de Vin sauce on top and keep warm in the oven. Slice the tomato thickly and place one slice on top of the sauce on each bread croûte and continue to keep warm. Reheat the eggs and drain well. Place one egg on top of each tomato slice. Spoon over some of the Hollandaise sauce and sprinkle with the bacon to serve. Serves 4.*

# Eggs Sardou

This traditional New Orleans brunch dish is still served in many restaurants. Hollandaise and other classic French sauces are used frequently in Creole cooking.

1½ pounds fresh spinach
1½ Tbsps butter or margarine
1 Tbsp flour
1 cup milk
Salt, pepper, and nutmeg
4 canned artichoke hearts, quartered
4 eggs

HOLLANDAISE SAUCE
3 egg yolks
1 Tbsp lemon juice
Pinch salt and pepper
⅔ cup unsalted butter
1 large piece canned pimiento, cut into thin strips

Strip the spinach leaves from the stalks and wash them well. Place in a large saucepan with a pinch of salt. Cover and cook over moderate heat in only the water that clings to the leaves. When it has just wilted, take off the heat and drain well. Chop roughly and set aside. Melt the butter in a medium saucepan and stir in the flour. Gradually add the milk, whisking constantly, and place over low heat. Whisk the sauce as it comes to a boil and boil rapidly for about 1 minute to thicken. Stir in the spinach and season with salt, pepper, and nutmeg. Add the artichoke hearts and set the sauce aside. Fill a large skillet with water and bring to a boil. Turn down the heat and, when the water is just barely simmering, break one egg at a time into a cup or onto a saucer. Gently lower into the water to poach over a gentle heat. Do not allow the water to boil. Cook until the whites have set but the yolks are still soft. Remove the eggs from the pan with a draining spoon and place in cold water until ready to use. To make the sauce, place the egg yolks in a blender with the lemon juice and seasoning. Process once or twice to mix. Melt the butter in a small saucepan over gentle heat. Turn up the heat and when the butter is bubbling, gradually pour onto the eggs in a very thin but steady stream with the machine running. To assemble the dish, reheat the spinach sauce and place an equal amount of it on four plates. Make a well in center. Place the eggs back into hot water briefly to reheat, and drain well. Place an egg in each hollow and spoon over some of the Hollandaise sauce to coat each egg completely. Make a cross with two strips of pimiento on top of each egg and serve immediately.
Serves 4.

*Above left: Antoine's, New Orleans' oldest restaurant, pictured in the 1890s. Right: children pose for a photograph beside the French Market, an area which still bustles with activity today.*

# Crawfish Pie

Crawfish are just one of the many shellfish available in and around New Orleans. This dish is one of those Louisiana specialties imortalized in that old song "Jambalaya" by Hank Williams.

### PASTRY
2 cups all-purpose flour, sifted
Pinch salt
½-¾ cup butter or margarine
Cold water
½ quantity spice mixture for Shellfish Boil (see page 40)
1 pound peeled, raw crawfish or shrimp

### FILLING
3 Tbsps oil
3 Tbsps flour
½ green bell pepper, finely diced
2 green onions, finely chopped
1 stalk celery, finely chopped
1 cup heavy cream
Salt and pepper

Sift the flour for the pastry into a bowl with a pinch of salt and cut in the butter or margarine until the mixture resembles fine bread crumbs. Add enough cold water to bring the mixture together. Knead into a ball, wrap well and chill for about 30 minutes before use. Combine the spice mixture in a saucepan with about 2½ cups water. Bring to a boil and add the crawfish or shrimp. Cook for about 5 minutes, stirring occasionally until the shellfish curl up. Remove from the liquid and leave to drain. Heat the oil for the filling in a small saucepan and add the flour. Cook slowly, stirring constantly until the flour turns a rich dark brown. Add the remaining filling ingredients, stirring constantly while adding the cream. Bring to a boil, reduce the heat and cook for about 5 minutes. Add the crawfish or shrimp to the sauce. Divide the dough into 4 and roll out each portion on a lightly-floured surface to about ¼-inch thick. Line individual pie pans with the dough, pushing it carefully onto the base and up the sides, taking care not to stretch it. Trim off excess dough and reserve. Place a sheet of baking parchment or foil on the dough and pour on rice, pasta or baking beans to come halfway up the sides. Bake the dough for about 10 minutes in a preheated 400° F oven. Remove the paper and beans and bake for an additional 5 minutes to cook the base. Spoon in the filling and roll out the trimmings to make a lattice pattern on top. Bake for 10 minutes to brown the lattice and heat the filling.
Serves 4.

# Red Beans and Rice

*This brunch dish was a favorite of Louis Armstrong, who at the end of a letter, would often sign himself as "Red beans and ricely yours!" This dish is often served on New Year's day, when it is associated with good luck.*

8 oz dried red kidney beans
1 sprig thyme
1 bay leaf
8 oz ham or bacon
¼ cup butter or margarine
1 onion, finely chopped
1 green bell pepper, cut into small dice
2 cloves garlic, minced
3 stalks celery, finely chopped
1 tsp cayenne pepper
Salt
8 oz rice, cooked, to serve
4 green onions, finely chopped

*Place the beans in a large stockpot or bowl, cover with water and leave to soak overnight. Drain them and place in a pot of fresh water with the thyme, bay leaf, and a pinch of salt. Add the piece of ham or bacon and bring to a boil. Partially cover the pan and boil rapidly for 10 minutes. Reduce the heat and then simmer for 1¼-1½ hours. Melt the butter in a small skillet and cook the onion, bell pepper, garlic, and celery until the onion looks translucent. Add this mixture to the beans and continue cooking them for 1¼-1½ hours longer, adding more water if necessary. Meanwhile, as soon as the beans are soft, mash some against the side of the pot with a large spoon. Remove the ham or bacon, trim it, and cut the meat into ½-inch pieces. Return to the beans and add cayenne pepper and salt. Stir well and continue cooking. Remove thyme and bay leaf before serving. Place hot rice on serving plates and spoon over some of the beans. Sprinkle the top with the chopped green onions. Serves 6-8.*

## Creole Eggplant

*Eggplant is a much-loved vegetable in Creole cooking, and is served in a variety of ways.*

2 eggplants
⅓ cup butter or margarine
1 onion, finely chopped
1 stalk celery, finely chopped
1 small red bell pepper, chopped
1 clove garlic, minced
Salt and pepper
4 oz cooked, peeled shrimp
Dry bread crumbs

*Cut the eggplants in half lengthwise and remove the stems. Score the cut surface lightly and sprinkle with salt. Leave to stand for 30 minutes, then rinse, pat dry and wrap in foil. Bake for 15 minutes in a preheated 350° F oven. Scoop out the center of the baked eggplants, leaving a ¼ inch of flesh inside the skins to form a shell. Chop the scooped out flesh roughly. Melt the butter in a pan and add the chopped eggplant, onion, celery, bell pepper, and garlic. Cook slowly to soften the vegetables. Season with salt and pepper, and add the shrimp. Spoon the mixture into the shells, sprinkle with bread crumbs and bake in an ovenproof dish for an additional 20 minutes. Serve hot. Serves 4.*

## Coush-Coush

*This Cajun invention makes a tasty brunch dish. Serve with fresh fruit or jam, milk and sugar, or syrup.*

1½ cups yellow cornmeal
4 Tbsps all-purpose flour
1 Tbsp baking powder
2 tsps sugar
Pinch salt
2½ cups water
⅓ cup butter or margarine

*Mix all the dry ingredients in a large bowl and add the water gradually, mixing until smooth. Melt the butter in a medium skillet and, when foaming, add the cornmeal mixture, spreading it out smoothly in the pan. Turn up the heat and fry until brown and crisp on the bottom. Stir the mixture to distribute the brown crust. Reduce the heat and cover the pan tightly. Cook for about 10-15 minutes, stirring occasionally. Spoon into serving bowls and serve hot. Serves 4-6.*

*Right: St. Charles Avenue, New Orleans, shortly before the arrival of the first motor car.*

# Sweet Potato and Sausage Casserole

Sweet potatoes are a favorite all over the Southern States. They are often made into sweet dishes with spices, and baked or served in pies. This savory dish is a bit like a soufflé but not as light.

2 pounds sweet potatoes, peeled
2 Tbsps oil
8 oz sausage meat
1 small onion, finely chopped
2 stalks celery, finely chopped
½ green bell pepper, finely chopped
Pinch sage and thyme
Pinch salt and pepper
2 eggs, separated

Cut the sweet potatoes into 2-inch pieces. Place in a saucepan of boiling water with a pinch of salt. Cook quickly, uncovered, for about 20 minutes or until tender. Drain well and leave to dry, then purée using a potato masher. While the sweet potatoes are cooking, heat the oil in a large skillet and add the sausage meat. Cook briskly, breaking up with a fork until it is golden brown. Add the onion, celery, and bell pepper, and cook another 5 minutes. Add the herbs and seasoning. Beat the egg yolks into the mashed sweet potatoes and, using an electric mixer, beat the egg whites until stiff but not dry. Drain off excess oil from the sausage meat before combining it with the sweet potatoes. Fold in the egg whites until thoroughly incorporated. Spoon the mixture into a well-buttered casserole or soufflé dish and bake in a preheated 375° F oven until risen and brown on the top – about 25-30 minutes. Serve immediately. Serves 6.

## Cajun Pies

These pies are spicy hot with cayenne pepper, one of the much used seasonings in Cajun cooking.

PASTRY
3 Tbsps butter or margarine
2 eggs
4-6 Tbsps milk or water
2½-3½ cups all-purpose flour
Pinch sugar and salt
FILLING
2 Tbsps butter or margarine
½ small onion, finely chopped
½ small green bell pepper, finely chopped
1 stalk celery, finely chopped
1 clove garlic, minced
¾ pound ground pork
1 bay leaf
1 tsp cayenne pepper
Pinch salt
2 Tbsps flour
1 cup beef stock
1 Tbsp tomato paste
1 tsp dried thyme

To prepare the pastry, soften the butter or margarine with an electric mixer until creamy. Beat in the eggs one at a time and add the milk or water. Sift in 2½ cups flour, the sugar, and salt and mix until blended. If necessary, add the remaining flour gradually until the mixture forms a ball. Wrap and refrigerate about 30 minutes. Melt the butter or margarine for the filling in a large skillet and cook the onion, bell pepper, celery, garlic, and pork over moderate heat. Break up the meat with a fork as it cooks. Add the bay leaf, cayenne pepper, salt, and flour. Cook, scraping the bottom of the pan often, until the flour browns. Stir in the stock, tomato paste, and thyme. Bring to a boil and cook, stirring occasionally, until thickened. Chill thoroughly and remove bay leaf. Divide pastry into 8 and roll each piece out to a circle about ⅛-inch thick. Spread the chilled filling on half of each circle to within ½ inch of the edge and brush the edge with water. Fold over and seal edges together firmly, then crimp with a fork. Heat oil in a deep sauté pan or a deep-fat fryer to about 350° F. Fry 2 or 3 pies at a time for about 2 minutes, holding them under the surface of the oil with a metal spoon to brown evenly. Remove from the oil with a draining spoon and drain on paper towels. Serve immediately.
Makes 8.

# CHAPTER THREE

# Fish and Seafood

*Above: at one time oysters were so plentiful they were sold from stands for a pittance. Today, it is the oyster bars that satisfy New Orleans enduring appetite for the delicacy.*

*Fish and seafood is the main-stay of Cajun and Creole cuisine, which is no wonder when you consider the geographical positioning of New Orleans. The bayous, the Gulf of Mexico, and Lake Pontchartrain supply the area with fresh fish and shellfish all year round. Crawfish, oysters, crab, jumbo shrimp, pompano, red snapper, and trout are the most popular and feature on numerous local menus. This natural abundance of fish and seafood has been essential to the survival of the local inhabitants in centuries gone by, for instance oysters were once so plentiful that the poor more or less lived on them, and indeed they would probably have starved without them.*

# Seafood Pan Roast

Such is the love of seafood that it is served in all shapes and forms. Here oysters and fresh crab are turned into a recipe that is based on the French gratin.

24 small oysters, on the half shell
1 cup fish stock
1 cup heavy cream
1 large or 2 small cooked crabs
4 slices bread, crusts trimmed, made into crumbs
1/3 cup butter or margarine
6 Tbsps flour
1 bunch green onions, chopped
2 oz parsley, chopped
2 Tbsps Worcestershire sauce
1/2 tsp Tabasco

Remove the oysters from their shells, place in a saucepan and strain over any oyster liquid. Add the fish stock and cook gently until the oysters curl around the edges. Remove the oysters, keep them warm and strain the liquid into a clean pan. Add the cream, bring to a boil and boil rapidly for about 5 minutes. Remove the crab's claws and legs. Turn the crab over and push out the body, remove the stomach sac and lungs and discard. Cut the body in four sections and pick out the meat with a skewer. Crack claws and legs to extract the meat. Scrape out the brown meat from inside the shell and combine it with the bread crumbs and white meat from the body and claws. Melt the butter in a medium saucepan and stir in the flour. Cook gently for 5 minutes. Add the onions and parsley and cook another 5 minutes. Pour over the cream mixture, stirring constantly, then bring to a boil. Add the Worcestershire sauce and Tabasco. Cook about 15-20 minutes over low heat, stirring occasionally. Fold in the crab meat mixture. Place the oysters in the bottom of a buttered casserole or in individual dishes and spoon the crab meat mixture on top. Broil to brown, if desired, and serve immediately. Serves 4.

## Shellfish Boil

One of the simplest Cajun ways of cooking shellfish is to boil it in a courtbouillon (water flavored with spices), then pile it up on to newspaper-covered tables for everyone to dig in.

3 quarts water
1 lemon, quartered
1 onion, cut in half but not peeled
1 stalk celery, cut in 3 pieces
2 cloves garlic, left whole
Pinch salt
4 bay leaves
1 Tbsp dill weed, fresh or dry
4 dried red chiles, crumbled
1 Tbsp each whole cloves, whole allspice, coriander seed and mustard seed (spice mix)
2 tsps celery seed
1 pound raw, unpeeled shrimp
2 pounds mussels, well scrubbed

Place the water, lemon, onion, celery, garlic, salt, herbs, and spices together in a large pot and cover. Bring to a boil, reduce the heat and cook slowly for 20 minutes. Add the shrimp in two batches and cook until pink and curled. Remove with a draining spoon. Add the mussels to the pot and cook, stirring frequently, for about 5 minutes or until shells have opened. Discard any that do not open. Spoon shrimp and mussels into serving bowls and serve immediately. Serves 4–6.

# Trout with Oyster Stuffing

*As oysters are so plentiful around New Orleans they are used freely in the local cooking.*

### Blackened Fish

*This dish was made famous in a New Orleans restaurant by the renowned Cajun chef Paul Prudhomme. The fish, usually redfish or pompano, should be cooked until it has a very brown crust.*

1 cup unsalted butter
4 fish fillets or steaks, eg. redfish or pompano, about 8 oz each
1 Tbsp paprika
1 tsp garlic powder
1 tsp cayenne pepper
½ tsp ground white pepper
1 tsp finely ground black pepper
2 tsps salt
1 tsp dried thyme

4 trout, about 8 oz each, cleaned
½ cup butter or margarine
1 onion, finely chopped
2 stalks celery, finely chopped
1 small red bell pepper, finely chopped
4 green onions, finely chopped
1 clove garlic, minced
12 oysters, on the half shell
¼ tsp each cayenne, white, and black pepper
1 tsp chopped fresh dill
2 tsps chopped parsley
1 cup dry bread crumbs
2 small eggs, lightly beaten

Wash the trout well. Melt half the butter in a medium saucepan. Add onion, celery, bell pepper, green onions, and garlic. Cook for about 3 minutes to soften the vegetables. Remove the oysters from the shells with a sharp knife. Strain and reserve any oyster liquid. Add the oysters to the pan, cook about 2 minutes, breaking them up into large pieces. Stir in the three kinds of pepper, dill, and parsley. Remove from the heat, add the bread crumbs and gradually beat in enough egg to hold the stuffing ingredients together. Season with salt. Fill the cavity of each trout with the stuffing and place in a baking dish. Spoon over the remaining butter and oyster liquid. Bake, uncovered, in a pre-heated 350° F oven for about 25 minutes. Brown under a pre-heated broiler before serving, if desired. Serves 4.

*Melt the butter and pour about half into each of four custard cups and set aside. Brush each fish fillet liberally with the remaining butter on both sides. Mix together the spices, seasonings, and thyme and sprinkle generously on each side of the fillets, patting it on by hand. Heat a skillet and add about 1 Tbsp butter per fish fillet. When the butter is hot, add the fish, skin side down first. Turn the fish over when the underside is very brown and repeat with the remaining side. Add more butter as necessary during cooking. When the top side of the fish is very dark brown, repeat with the remaining fish fillets, keeping them warm while cooking the rest. Serve the fish immediately with the cups of butter for dipping. Serves 4.*

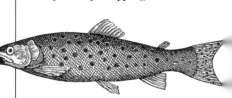

*Above left: oyster dredges line the wharf in New Orleans at the turn of the century. The once-plentiful supply of oysters has now dwindled, but the South is still the United States' principal oyster-producing region.*

# Creole Court Bouillon

*The name given to this classic Creole soup-stew refers to the sauce, which is based on fresh fish stock.*

2 whole whitefish, filleted and skinned, skin
and bones reserved
1 bay leaf, 1 sprig thyme and 2 parsley stalks
2 slices onion
1 lemon slice
6 black peppercorns
1½ cups water
6 Tbsps oil
6 Tbsps flour
1 large green bell pepper, finely chopped
1 onion, finely chopped
1 stalk celery, finely chopped
2 pounds canned tomatoes
2 Tbsps tomato paste
1 tsp cayenne pepper
Pinch salt and allspice
6 Tbsps white wine
2 Tbsps chopped parsley

Use the fish skin and bones, herbs, onion and lemon slices, peppercorns, and water to prepare the fish stock following the method for Poisson en Papillote (see page 50). Heat the oil in a large saucepan and add the flour. Cook slowly, stirring constantly, until golden brown. Add the bell pepper, onion, and celery. Cook until the flour is a rich dark brown and the vegetables have softened. Strain on the stock, stirring constantly. Add the canned tomatoes, tomato paste, cayenne pepper, salt and allspice. Bring to a boil and simmer until thick. Add the wine. Cut the fish fillets into 2-inch pieces and add to the tomato mixture. Cook slowly for about 20 minutes, or until the fish is tender. Gently stir in the parsley, taking care that the fish does not break up. Serves 4.

## Seafood Gumbo Filé

*Filé gumbo gets its name from the use of filé powder – a thickening agent made from the dried aromatic leaves of the sassafras tree, a relative of the bay tree.*

1 pound cooked, unpeeled shrimp
½ quantity spice mixture for
Shellfish Boil (see page 40)
5 cups water
4 Tbsps butter or margarine
1 onion, sliced
1 green bell pepper, sliced
2 cloves garlic, minced
3 Tbsps flour
½ tsp thyme
1 bay leaf
2 Tbsps chopped parsley
Dash Worcestershire sauce
12 oysters, shelled
8 oz tomatoes, peeled and chopped
2 Tbsps filé powder
Salt and pepper
Cooked rice, to serve

Peel the shrimp and reserve the shells. Mix the shells with the spice mixture and water, bring to a boil in a large stock pot. Reduce the heat and simmer for 20 minutes. Melt the butter in a large saucepan. When foaming, add the onion, bell pepper, garlic, and flour. Cook slowly, stirring constantly until the flour is pale golden brown. Gradually strain on the stock, discarding the shells and spice mixture. Add the thyme and bay leaf and stir well. Bring to a boil and then simmer until thick. Add the parsley, Worcestershire sauce, oysters, peeled shrimp and tomatoes. Heat through gently to cook the oysters. Stir in the filé powder and leave to stand to thicken. Adjust the seasoning and serve over hot rice. Serves 6.

# New Orleans Jambalaya

*There are countless versions of this spicy soup-stew. Its
origins have been likened to the Spanish dish Paella.*

## Crawfish Étouffée

*This Cajun specialty is a thick
peppery stew that is served with rice.
Other shellfish such as shrimp can
also be used.*

1/3 cup butter or margarine
1 small onion, chopped
1 pound crawfish
6 Tbsps flour·
1 cup water or fish stock
1 Tbsp tomato paste
1 Tbsp chopped parsley
2 tsps chopped dill
2 tsps Tabasco or to taste
Salt and black pepper
Cooked rice, to serve

Melt half the butter or margarine in
a saucepan, add the onion and
cook to soften slightly. Add crawfish
and cook quickly until it curls.
Remove to a plate. Add the flour to
the pan and cook slowly until
golden brown, stirring frequently.
Pour on the water and stir
vigorously to blend. Add tomato
paste and bring to a boil. Add
parsley, dill, Tabasco, salt, and
plenty of pepper, and return the
onions and crawfish to the sauce.
Heat through for 5 minutes and
serve over hot rice. Serves 4.

2 Tbsps butter or margarine
2 Tbsps flour
1 medium onion, finely chopped
1 clove garlic, minced
1 red bell pepper, finely chopped
14 oz canned tomatoes
4 cups fish or chicken stock
1/4 tsp ground ginger
Pinch of allspice
1 tsp chopped fresh thyme or 1/2 tsp dried thyme
1/4 tsp cayenne pepper
Pinch of salt
Dash of Tabasco
4 oz uncooked rice
2 pounds uncooked shrimp, peeled
2 green onions, chopped, to garnish

Melt the butter in a heavy-based saucepan and then add
the flour. Stir to blend well and cook over low heat until a
pale straw color. Add the onion, garlic, and bell pepper
and cook until soft. Add the tomatoes and their juice,
breaking them up with a fork or a potato masher. Add
the stock and mix well. Add the ginger, allspice, thyme,
cayenne pepper, salt, and Tabasco. Bring to a boil and
allow to boil rapidly for about 2 minutes, stirring. Add
the rice, stir well, and cover the pan. Cook for about
15-20 minutes, or until the rice is tender and has
absorbed most of the liquid. Add the shrimp during the
last 10 minutes of cooking time. Cook until the shrimp
curl and turn pink. Adjust the seasoning, spoon into a
serving dish and sprinkle with the chopped green onions
to serve. Serves 4-6.

*Above left: St. Louis Cathedral,
grandly presiding over Jackson
Square. Built in the Spanish
style and dating from 1789 it
is the third church to stand on
this site and is the oldest active
cathedral in the United States.*

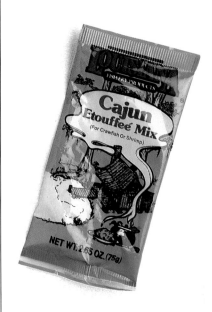

# Shrimp Creole

*Shrimp Creole, or Shrimp Sauce Piquante as it is also called in New Orleans, is based on a spicy reddish-brown gravy. The local cooks also use this sauce to serve with other meat such as chicken, alligator and frog legs.*

## Barbecued Shrimp

*The name refers to the sauce rather than the method of cooking. Whole jumbo shrimp are cooked in a spicy hot butter and garlic sauce. Eat them with your fingers.*

*1 pound jumbo shrimp, cooked and unpeeled*
*½ cup unsalted butter*
*1 tsp each white, black and cayenne pepper*
*1 tsp each chopped fresh thyme, rosemary and marjoram*
*1 clove garlic, minced*
*1 tsp Worcestershire sauce*
*½ cup fish stock*
*4 Tbsps dry white wine*
*Pinch salt*
*Cooked rice, to serve*

*Remove the eyes and the legs from the shrimp. Melt the butter in a large skillet and add the three kinds of pepper, herbs, and garlic. Add the shrimp and toss over heat for a few minutes. Remove the shrimp and set them aside. Add the Worcestershire sauce, stock, and wine to the ingredients in the pan. Bring to a boil and cook for about 3 minutes to reduce. Add salt to taste. Arrange the shrimp on a bed of hot rice and pour over the sauce to serve. Serves 2.*

*4 Tbsps oil*
*1 large green bell pepper, cut into 1-inch pieces*
*2 stalks celery, sliced*
*2 medium onions, diced*
*2 cloves garlic, minced*
*2 × 14 oz cans tomatoes*
*2 bay leaves*
*1 tsp cayenne pepper or Tabasco*
*Pinch of salt and pepper*
*Pinch of thyme*
*2 Tbsps cornstarch mixed with 3 Tbsps dry white wine*
*1½ pounds shrimp, uncooked*
*Cooked rice, to serve*

*Place the oil in a large saucepan and add the bell pepper, celery, and onions. Cook for a few minutes over gentle heat and add the garlic. Add the tomatoes and their juice, breaking them up with a fork or a potato masher. Add the bay leaves, cayenne pepper or Tabasco, seasoning, and thyme, and bring to a boil. Allow to simmer for about 5 minutes, uncovered. Mix a few spoonfuls of the hot tomato liquid with the cornstarch mixture and then return it to the saucepan. Bring to a boil, stirring constantly until thickened. Add the shrimp and cover the pan. Simmer over gentle heat for about 20 minutes, or until the shrimp curl and look pink and opaque. Remove the bay leaves before serving, and spoon the sauce over hot rice. Serves 4.*

*Above left: this fascinating view across the busy Mississippi towards New Orleans is taken from an 1848 hand-colored wood engraving.*

# Poisson en Papillote

This famous New Orleans dish, most often prepared with pompano, makes an impressive main course dish. The parchment parcels should be opened at the table.

4 double or 8 single whitefish fillets
Fishbones and trimmings
1 bay leaf, sprig thyme, and 2 parsley stalks
6 black peppercorns
1 slice lemon
1 cup dry white wine
1 cup water
4 large sheets of baking parchment
8 uncooked jumbo shrimp, shelled
4 crab claws, cracked and shelled
¼ cup butter or margarine
3 Tbsps flour
1 onion, finely chopped
Pinch salt and pepper
2 egg yolks

To make fish stock, skin the fish fillets and place the skin in a large stockpot along with the fish bones, bay leaf, thyme, parsley, peppercorns, and lemon slice. Add the wine and water and bring to a boil. Lower the heat and simmer for 20 minutes. Strain and set aside. Cut the baking parchment into large ovals big enough to form a parcel for each double fish fillet, or 2 single fillets. Fold the paper in half, then open out and lightly oil. Place the fish on one half of the paper and arrange the shrimp and crab claws on top. Melt the butter in a heavy-based saucepan and, when foaming, add the flour. Cook for 2-3 minutes, stirring frequently until a pale straw color. Add the onion and cook until lightly browned. Gradually pour on the fish stock, whisking continuously. Bring to a boil, then cook over moderate heat for 4-5 minutes, or until thickened. Season to taste. Mix the egg yolks with a few spoonfuls of the hot sauce and then stir into the sauce. Spoon some of the sauce over each fillet, fold the paper over to cover, and seal the edges, folding over twice and twisting the ends slightly to seal completely. Place the parcels on cookie sheets and place in a preheated 400° F oven for about 20 minutes. Serve any remaining sauce separately. Serves 4.

*Above left: a Spanish fort pavilion built near New Orleans during the period of Spanish rule. Right: Steamboats were once a major form of transport on the Mississippi.*

# CHAPTER FOUR

# Meat and Poultry

*Above: Royal Street, with its interesting old buildings, runs the width of the French Quarter.*

Game such as deer, rabbit, squirrel, duck, pigeon, turkey, and goose played an important role in the early recipes of Cajun and Creole cuisine. And while Cajun recipes still tend to use the cheaper cuts of meat, such as oxtail, and neck of lamb, the more sophisticated cuisine of the Creoles uses finer cuts such as steak. Local meat specialties include andouille and boudin, both types of well flavored sausages, and tasso, a type of smoked ham. Flavorings are all important additions to food, and in Cajun cooking a mixture of three kinds of pepper – red (cayenne), white, and black – is used to give the traditional dishes their distinctive taste. Another essential basic is roux gravy; derived from the French roux sauce this is the foundation of many classic Creole and Cajun dishes and involves the long slow cooking of flour and butter to a rich brown color.

53

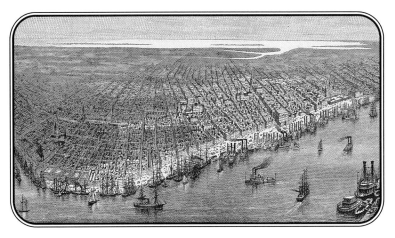

# Chicken Gumbo

½ cup oil
3 pound chicken, cut into 6-8 pieces
1 cup flour
2-3 dried red chiles or 1-2 fresh chiles
1 large onion, finely chopped
1 large green bell pepper, roughly chopped
3 stalks celery, finely chopped
2 cloves garlic, minced
8 oz andouille sausage or garlic sausage, diced
4 cups chicken stock
1 bay leaf
Dash of Tabasco
Salt and pepper
4 oz fresh okra, trimmed
Cooked rice, to serve

Gumbo is a popular New Orleans dish, and gets its name from "gombo," the African word for okra – the vegetable on which the dish was originally based.

*Above: houses with pretty wrought-iron balconies are characteristic of the French Quarter. Above right: an aerial view of New Orleans, showing Lake Ponchartrain in the distance. Levees can be seen along the edge of the river; these had to be built to protect the city, which stands six feet below sea level, from the waters of the Mississippi.*

Heat the oil in a large skillet and brown the chicken on both sides, 3-4 pieces at a time. Transfer the chicken to a plate and set it aside. Add the flour to the pan and cook over a very low heat for about 30 minutes. Stir constantly until the flour turns a rich, dark brown. Take the pan off the heat occasionally, so that the flour does not burn. Add the chiles, onion, bell pepper, celery, garlic, and sausage to the roux and cook for about 5 minutes over very low heat, stirring continuously. Pour on the stock and stir well. Add the bay leaf, Tabasco, and salt and pepper, then bring to a boil. Reduce the heat and return the chicken to the pan. Cover and cook for about 30 minutes or until the chicken is tender. Cut each okra into 2-3 pieces. If okra are small, leave whole. Add to the chicken and cook for another 10-15 minutes. Remove the bay leaf and serve the Gumbo over hot rice. Serves 4-6.

# Fried Chicken Creole

*A sauce flavored with garlic, herbs and wine is the Creole addition to Southern-Fried Chicken.*

Flour for dredging
Salt and pepper
3 pound frying chicken, cut into 12 serving pieces
6 Tbsps oil
5 Tbsps butter or margarine
1 clove garlic, minced
1 small onion, finely chopped
4 oz bacon or uncooked ham, diced
6 tomatoes, peeled and chopped
2 tsps fresh thyme or 1 tsp dried thyme
½ cup white wine
2 Tbsps chopped parsley

*Above right: Mardi Gras is the year's most anticipated event in New Orleans, and attracts tourists from all over the world. A popular feature of the parades and street dancing are the "krewes," who throw glass beads and trinkets to the crowds. Facing page: this absorbing old photograph is of Canal Street, the uptown boundary of the French Quarter, and one of the widest avenues in the world.*

Mix the flour with salt and pepper and dredge the chicken lightly, shaking the pieces to remove any excess flour. Heat the oil in a large skillet and add the butter. Add the chicken drumstick and thigh pieces skin side down and allow to brown over moderately low heat so that the chicken cooks as well as browns. Turn and brown on the other side. Push to one side of the pan, add the breast meat, and brown in the same way. Add the garlic, onion, and bacon or ham and lower the heat. Cook slowly for about 10 minutes, or until the bacon browns slightly. Add the tomatoes, seasoning, and thyme and lower the heat. Cook until the chicken is tender and the tomatoes are softened. Using a draining spoon, transfer the chicken and other ingredients to a serving dish and keep warm. Remove all but about 4 Tbsps of the oil from the pan and deglaze with the wine, scraping up the browned bits from the bottom. Bring to a boil and allow to reduce slightly. Pour over the chicken and sprinkle with parsley. Serves 6.

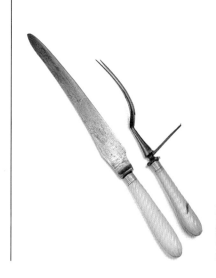

56

# Chicken with Cajun Stuffing

*In this recipe, two favorite Cajun ingredients, smoked ham and eggplant, make a rich and tasty stuffing.*

*3 pound roasting chicken*
*2 Tbsps butter, softened*

STUFFING
*1 small eggplant*
*2 Tbsps butter or margarine*
*2 shallots, finely chopped*
*4 oz smoked ham, chopped*
*1½ cups fresh bread crumbs*
*1 tsp chopped fresh thyme*
*1 tsp chopped fresh oregano*
*2 tsps chopped parsley*
*Pinch cayenne pepper*
*1-2 eggs, beaten*
*Salt and pepper*

*To prepare the stuffing, cut the eggplant in half lengthwise and remove stem. Lightly score the surface with a knife and sprinkle with salt. Leave to stand for about 30 minutes. Melt the butter in a medium saucepan and when foaming, add the shallots. Cook slowly to soften slightly. Rinse the eggplant and pat dry. Cut into ½-inch cubes. Cook with the shallot until fairly soft then remove from the heat. Add the remaining stuffing ingredients, beating in enough egg so the mixture just holds together. Season to taste. Fill the chicken cavity with the stuffing, securing the opening with skewers. Tie the legs together, place the chicken in a roasting pan and spread over the softened butter. Roast in a pre-heated 375° F oven for about 1½ hours, or until the juices run clear when the thickest part of the thigh is pierced with a sharp knife. Leave the chicken to stand for 10 minutes before carving. If desired, make a gravy with the pan juices. Serves 4-6.*

### Chicken St. Pierre

*This Southern combination of chicken, lima beans, peppers, and onions gets the French treatment in this Creole stew.*

*1 × 3 pound chicken*
*⅓ cup butter or margarine*
*3 Tbsps flour*
*1 large red bell pepper, diced*
*1 large green bell pepper, diced*
*6 green onions, chopped*
*½ cup dry white wine*
*1 cup chicken stock*
*6 oz lima beans*
*1 tsp chopped thyme*
*Salt, pepper and pinch nutmeg*
*Dash of Tabasco (optional)*

*Cut the chicken into 8 pieces, removing the legs first. Cut between the legs and the body of the chicken. Bend the legs backwards to break the joint and cut away from the body. Cut the drumstick and thigh joints in half. Cut down the breastbone with a sharp knife and then use poultry shears to cut through the bone and ribcage to remove the breast joints from the back. Cut both breast joints in half, leaving some white meat attached to the wing joint. Heat the butter in a large skillet and when foaming add the chicken, skin side down.*

*Brown on one side, turn over and brown other side. Remove the chicken and add the flour to the pan. Cook to a pale straw color. Add the bell peppers and onions and cook briefly. Pour on the wine and chicken stock and bring to a boil. Stir constantly until thickened. Add the chicken, lima beans, thyme, seasoning, and nutmeg. Cover the pan and cook about 25 minutes, or until the chicken is tender. Add Tabasco to taste, if desired, before serving. Serves 4-6.*

## Pecan Chicken

*Pecans are native to this region and are a variety of the hickory nut. They are used in savory dishes as well as sweet.*

*4 boned chicken breasts*
*3 Tbsps butter or margarine*
*1 small onion, finely chopped*
*3 oz pork sausage meat*
*3 oz fresh bread crumbs*
*1 tsp chopped thyme*
*1 tsp chopped parsley*
*Salt and pepper*
*1 small egg, lightly beaten*
*1 cup pecan halves*
*1 cup chicken stock*
*1 Tbsp flour*
*2 Tbsps sherry*
*Chopped parsley or 1 bunch watercress, to garnish*

*Cut a small pocket in the thick side of each chicken breast using a small knife. Melt 1 Tbsp butter in a small saucepan and add the onion. Cook a few minutes over gentle heat to soften. Add the sausage meat and turn up the heat to brown. Break up the sausage meat with a fork as it cooks. Drain off any fat and add the bread crumbs, herbs, and a pinch of salt and pepper. Allow to cool slightly and add enough egg to hold the mixture*

# Fried Chicken

*Fried Chicken is **the** dish associated with the South. Everyone has their own recipe, which they claim is the best.*

*3 pounds frying chicken portions*
*2 eggs*
*2 cups flour*
*1 tsp each salt, paprika and sage*
*½ tsp black pepper*
*Pinch cayenne pepper*
*Oil for frying*
*Parsley or watercress*

*Rinse the chicken and pat dry. Beat the eggs in a large bowl and add the chicken one piece at a time, turning to coat. Mix flour and seasoning in a large plastic bag. Place chicken pieces coated with egg into the bag one at a time, close bag tightly and shake to coat each piece of chicken. Heat oil in a large skillet to the depth of about ½ inch. When hot, add the chicken skin side down first. Fry about 12 minutes and then turn over. Fry a further 12 minutes or until the juices run clear. Drain the chicken on paper towels and serve immediately. Garnish serving plate with parsley or watercress. Serves 4.*

*together. Chop pecans, reserving 8, and add to the meat. Using a small teaspoon, fill the pocket in each chicken breast with some of the meat. Melt 1 Tbsp butter in a casserole and place in the chicken breasts, skin side down first. Brown over moderate heat and turn over. Brown the other side quickly to seal.*

*Pour in the stock, cover the casserole and cook for about 25-30 minutes in a preheated 350° F oven. When chicken is cooked, remove it to a serving plate to keep warm. Reserve cooking liquid. Melt remaining butter in a small saucepan and stir in the flour. Cook to a pale straw color. Strain on the cooking liquid and add the sherry. Bring to a boil and stir constantly until thickened. Add the reserved pecans. Spoon some of the sauce over the chicken. Garnish with chopped parsley or a bouquet of watercress. Serves 4.*

# Squabs in Wine

*All sorts of game are used in Cajun cookery, as the countryside surrounding New Orleans is the perfect habitat for many species.*

*4 squabs*
*½ tsp each cayenne, white, and black pepper*
*Pinch of salt*
*2 Tbsps oil*
*2 Tbsps butter or margarine*
*12 oz button onions, peeled*
*2 stalks celery, sliced*
*4 carrots, peeled and sliced*
*4 Tbsps flour*
*1½ cups chicken stock*
*½ cup dry red wine*
*2 tsps tomato paste (optional)*
*4 oz mushrooms, quartered or left whole if small*
*3 oz fresh or frozen lima beans*
*2 Tbsps chopped parsley*

*Wipe the squabs and season the cavities with the three kinds of pepper and a pinch of salt. Heat the oil in a heavy-based casserole and add the butter. Once it is foaming, place in the squabs, two at a time if necessary. Brown them on all sides, turning frequently. Remove from the casserole and set aside. Add the onions, celery, and carrots to the casserole and cook for about 5 minutes to brown slightly. Add the flour and cook until golden brown, stirring constantly. Pour in the stock and the wine and stir well. Bring to a boil over high heat until thickened. Stir in the tomato paste, if using, and return the squabs to the casserole along with any liquid that has accumulated. Partially cover the casserole and simmer gently for about 40-45 minutes, or until the squabs are tender. Add the mushrooms and lima beans halfway through cooking time. Sprinkle with parsley. Serves 4.*

*Above: a magnificent town house on St. Charles Avenue. The street boasts an array of grand homes, many built by wealthy plantation owners.*

### Paneed Lemon Veal

*Paneed is the Creole word for pan-fried. This method of cooking is used for tender cuts of veal, chicken or beef. Quite often the meat is coated in a layer of seasoned bread crumbs, before being fried until crunchy-crisp on the outside.*

*8 veal cutlets*
*Flour for dredging*
*Salt and pepper*
*2 Tbsps butter or margarine*
*1 green bell pepper, thinly sliced*
*6 Tbsps dry white wine*
*1 Tbsp lemon juice*
*¾ cup chicken stock*
*1 lemon, skin and pith removed, and flesh thinly sliced*

*Dredge the veal with a mixture of flour, salt, and pepper. Shake off the excess. Melt the butter or margarine in a large skillet and brown the veal, a few pieces at a time. Remove the meat and keep it warm. Add the bell pepper to the pan and cook briefly then set aside with the veal. Pour the wine and lemon juice into the pan. Add the stock and bring to a boil. Boil for 5 minutes to reduce. Add the veal and pepper and cook 15 minutes over gentle heat. Add the lemon and heat through before serving. Serves 4.*

# Gingersnap Pork Chops

*Cajun cooking often uses whatever is to hand, and this unlikely combination of cookies and pork works very well. The ginger flavor gives a spicy lift to the gravy and thickens it at the same time.*

### Veal Jardinière

*This Creole-French recipe uses fresh, young, tender vegetables to accompany veal, which is, according to the recipe title, cooked the way of a gardener's wife.*

*2 Tbsps oil*
*4 large veal chops, trimmed*
*1 Tbsp butter or margarine*
*12 button onions, peeled*
*1 carrot, peeled and diced*
*1 Tbsp flour*
*1½ cups beef stock*
*6 Tbsps white wine*
*Salt and pepper*
*3 oz green beans, trimmed and sliced*
*2 oz peas*

*Heat the oil in a large skillet. Sauté the chops on both sides in the hot oil until browned. Melt the butter or margarine in a medium saucepan, and add the onions and carrot. Cook slowly to soften. Sprinkle on the flour and stirring constantly, cook slowly to a good golden brown. Add the stock, wine, salt, and pepper and bring to a boil. Cook until thick. Pour the fat from the veal and pour the sauce into the pan. Add the beans and peas and cook until the veal is tender – about 25 minutes. Serves 4.*

*4 even-sized pork chops, loin or shoulder*
*1 tsp ground black pepper*
*Pinch of salt*
*Pinch of dried thyme*
*¼ tsp each rubbed sage, cayenne pepper, ground coriander, and paprika*
*1 tsp ground ginger*
*2 Tbsps oil*
*2 Tbsps butter*
*1 small onion, finely chopped*
*1 stalk celery, finely chopped*
*½ clove garlic, minced*
*1½ cups chicken stock*
*12-14 gingersnap cookies*

*Trim the chops. Mix together the seasoning, herbs, and spices and press the mixture firmly onto the chops on both sides. Heat the oil in a large skillet and add the chops. Brown on both sides and remove to a plate. Add the butter to the pan and when foaming, add the onion, celery, and garlic. Cook to soften and pour on the stock. Return the chops to the pan, cover and cook for about 30-40 minutes, or until tender. When the chops are tender remove them to a serving dish and keep warm. Crush the gingersnaps in a food processor, or place them in a plastic bag and use a rolling pin to crush. Stir the crumbs into the pan liquid and bring to a boil. Stir constantly to allow the gingersnaps to soften and thicken the liquid. Boil rapidly for about 3 minutes to reduce, and pour over the chops to serve. Serves 4.*

*Although both Cajun and Creole cooking have French roots, as well as other major influences, the two cuisines can be easily distinguished from each other. Creole is the city cuisine, where cooks often competed to make complicated and fancy dishes using the finest foods available. Cajun cooking, on the other hand, has always been a much more basic, country-oriented cuisine, as people had to eke out a living from the land and make-do with what was available.*

# Spiced Lamb

*In New Orleans, being able to make a good roux is synonymous with being a good cook.*

*1 pound lamb neck fillets*
*1 tsp each chopped, fresh dill and thyme*
*1 tsp rosemary, crushed*
*2 bay leaves*
*2 tsps mustard seeds, lightly crushed*
*½ tsp ground allspice*
*1 tsp coarsely ground black pepper*
*Juice of 2 lemons*
*1 cup red wine*
*2 Tbsps oil*
*1 small red bell pepper, sliced*
*3 oz button mushrooms, left whole*
*2 Tbsps butter or margarine*
*3 Tbsps flour*
*½ cup beef stock*

*Place the lamb in a shallow dish and sprinkle on the herbs, spices, pepper, lemon juice, and wine, and stir to coat the meat thoroughly. Leave for 4 hours in the refrigerator. Heat the oil in a large skillet and add the bell pepper and mushrooms and cook to soften slightly. Remove with a draining spoon. Drain and dry the lamb, reserving the marinade. Add the meat to the pan and brown quickly on all sides. Remove from the pan and set aside with the vegetables. Melt the butter in the pan and when foaming add the flour. Lower the heat and cook the flour slowly until a good, rich brown. Stir in the stock and marinade. Bring to a boil, season and return the vegetables and lamb to the pan. Cook about 15 minutes, or until the lamb is tender, but still pink inside. Slice the lamb thinly on the diagonal and arrange on plates. Remove the bay leaves from the sauce and spoon over the meat. Serves 4.*

## Backbone Stew

*The mixture of cayenne, white, and black pepper is a typical Cajun addition to many savory dishes. This stew can also be made with pork chops.*

*3 pounds lamb chops; blade, rib or loin*
*¼ tsp each cayenne, white, and black pepper*
*Pinch of salt*
*6 Tbsps oil*
*2 onions, sliced*
*1 large red bell pepper, sliced*
*2 stalks celery, sliced*
*6 Tbsps flour*
*2 cloves garlic, minced*
*5 cups stock or water*
*2 Tbsps chopped parsley*

*Cut the lamb between the bones into individual pieces. Sprinkle a mixture of red, white, and black pepper, and salt over the surface of the chops, patting it in well. Heat the oil in a large stock pot or casserole and when hot add the meat, a few pieces at a time, and brown on both sides. When all the meat is brown, remove to a plate and add the onions, bell pepper, and celery to the oil. Lower the heat and cook to soften. Remove and set aside with the meat. Add the flour to the remaining oil in the pan and stir well. Cook slowly until a dark golden brown. Add the garlic and stir in the stock or water. Return the meat and vegetables to the pan or casserole and bring to a boil. Cover and cook slowly for 1½-2 hours, or until the lamb is very tender. Sprinkle with parsley and serve immediately. Serves 8.*

# Creole Oxtails

*This rich-flavored casserole makes use of one of the economical cuts of beef.*

*4½ pounds oxtails, cut into 2-inch pieces*
*Flour for dredging*
*Salt and pepper*
*2 Tbsps oil*
*2 onions, coarsely chopped*
*1 large green bell pepper, coarsely chopped*
*3 stalks celery, coarsely chopped*
*4 cloves garlic, minced*
*2 pounds canned tomatoes*
*2 cups beef stock*
*2 Tbsps red wine vinegar*
*2 Tbsps dark brown sugar*
*Pinch dried thyme*
*1 bay leaf*
*Pinch cayenne pepper*
*1 Tbsp Creole or Dijon mustard*
*Dash of Tabasco*
*Chopped parsley, to garnish*

*Trim off and discard any excess fat from the oxtail. Place a few pieces of oxtail at a time in a sieve and sprinkle over flour, salt, and pepper. Shake the sieve to coat. Heat the oil in a large casserole and brown the meat in several batches. When all the pieces are browned, remove to a plate and add the onions, bell pepper, celery, and garlic to the casserole. Cook over moderate heat, stirring until the vegetables have softened but not browned. Return the oxtail to the pan and add the tomatoes, stock, vinegar, brown sugar, thyme, bay leaf, and cayenne pepper. Bring to a boil and reduce the heat. Cover and cook gently on top of the stove or in a preheated 350° F oven for about 3½ hours, or until the meat is very tender. When the oxtail is cooked, transfer to a serving dish and remove the bay leaf from the sauce. Skim the sauce for any oil, and purée the vegetables and the sauce in a food processor until smooth. Add the mustard, Tabasco, and a pinch of salt, if necessary. Spoon over the oxtails and sprinkle with chopped parsley. Serves 8.*

## Grillades

*The roux sauce made in this recipe is ubiquitous in Creole and Cajun cooking. The classic French roux became the rich, brown Creole gravies that are cooked with so many of their specialty dishes.*

*4-8 pieces frying steak, depending on size*
*1 Tbsp oil*
*1 Tbsp butter or margarine*
*1 Tbsp flour*
*6 green onions*
*1 clove garlic, minced*
*1 tsp chopped thyme*
*2 tsps chopped parsley*
*3 tomatoes, peeled, seeded and chopped*
*1 cup beef stock*
*Dash of Tabasco*
*Salt*

*Place the meat between 2 sheets of waxed paper and pound with a rolling pin or meat mallet to flatten slightly. Heat the oil in a large skillet and brown the meat quickly, a few pieces at a time. Set the meat aside. Melt the butter or margarine in the skillet and add the flour. Cut the white part off the green onions and chop it finely. Add to the flour and butter, reserving the green tops for later use. Add garlic to the pan and cook the mixture slowly, stirring frequently until it is a dark golden brown. Add the herbs, tomatoes, stock, Tabasco, and salt to taste and bring to a boil. Cook about 5 minutes to thicken and add the steaks. Cook to heat the meat through. Chop the green tops of the onions and sprinkle over the steaks to garnish. Serves 4.*

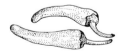

*Right: Dumaine Street. On this street stands a house with the strange name of "Madame John's Legacy." Believed to have been built around 1727, it was New Orleans author George Washington Cable who gave it its name in a short story.*

# CHAPTER FIVE

# Side Dishes and Salads

*Above: this evocative engraving from 1858 shows people enjoying a picnic in the woods surrounding New Orleans.*

*The vegetables most often used in Cajun and Creole cooking are tomatoes, corn, peppers, collard greens, sweet potatoes and yams, eggplants, and okra. The slave trade brought with it from Africa okra, collard greens, yams, and also black-eyed peas, which the black cooks soon learned to combine with local ingredients to create hearty new dishes. Salads, often based on eggs or seafood, rely on readily available vegetables that are in season for maximum freshness. The main staples, rice and corn, are also locally grown. Corn was cultivated by the native Powhatan Indians and it was they who introduced the first settlers to the variety of dishes which they made from the ground up grain. From these humble beginnings corn became the main staple of the whole of the South and has been its most vital food source throughout the centuries.*

## Maque Choux

Corn is cooked in many ways and forms. This Cajun recipe combines it with tomatoes and a creamy sauce.

4 Tbsps oil
2 Tbsps butter or margarine
2 medium onions, finely chopped
1 clove garlic, minced
1 medium green bell pepper, cut in small dice
6 tomatoes, peeled, seeded and diced
8 oz fresh corn kernels
1 cup chicken or vegetable stock
½ tsp cayenne pepper
Pinch of salt
¼ cup heavy cream

Heat the oil in a large casserole and add the butter. When foaming, add the onions, and garlic. Cook, stirring frequently, for about 5 minutes or until soft and transparent. Add the bell pepper, tomatoes, corn, and stock. Bring to a boil over high heat. Reduce the heat, partially cover the casserole and allow to cook slowly for about 10 minutes, or until the corn is tender. Add the cayenne pepper and salt and stir in the cream. Heat through and serve immediately. Serves 6.

# Creole Tomatoes

This recipe pays hommage to that classic taste of summer – the fresh, sun-ripened tomato. Garlic, wine, and cream make the perfect sauce with which to accompany them.

4 large ripe tomatoes, peeled
1 small green bell pepper, thinly sliced
4 green onions, sliced
1 clove garlic, minced
4 Tbsps white wine
Pinch cayenne pepper
Salt
1 Tbsp butter or margarine
4 Tbsps heavy cream

Cut the tomatoes in half and scoop out the seeds. Strain the juice and reserve it, discarding the seeds. Place tomatoes cut side down in a baking dish and sprinkle over the reserved juice. Add the bell pepper, onions, garlic, wine, cayenne pepper, and salt. Dot with butter or margarine. Place in a preheated 350° F oven for about 15-20 minutes, or until tomatoes are heated through and just tender. Strain the juices into a small saucepan and bring to a boil to reduce slightly. Stir in the cream and reboil. Spoon over the tomatoes to serve. Serves 4.

*Above left: the graceful courtyard of Brulatour Court on Royal Street. The house was built in 1816 by a French furniture maker and wine merchant.*

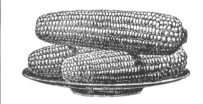

# Hot Pepper Egg Salad

*Eggs make popular salad, lunch and brunch dishes in Cajun and Creole cooking. Here the Cajun touch is adding a dressing laced with chile.*

## Green Rice

*Rice combined with lashings of chopped fresh herbs makes an excellent side dish to serve with any meat, poultry or game. Use whatever herbs complement the main course.*

2 Tbsps oil
2 Tbsps butter
¾ cup uncooked long-grain rice
2 cups boiling water
Pinch salt and pepper
3 oz mixed fresh herbs (parsley, thyme, marjoram, basil), finely chopped
1 small bunch green onions, finely chopped

4 eggs
½ bunch of green onions, chopped
½ small red bell pepper, chopped
½ small green bell pepper, chopped
4 oz cooked, peeled shrimp
1 small jar artichoke hearts, drained and quartered
Shredded lettuce, to serve

DRESSING
6 Tbsps oil
2 Tbsps white wine vinegar
1 clove garlic, minced
1 tsp dry mustard
1-2 tsps hot red pepper flakes, or 1 small fresh chile, seeded and finely chopped
Salt

*Prick the large end of the eggs with an egg pricker or a needle, and lower carefully into boiling, salted water. Bring back to a boil, rolling the eggs in the water with the bowl of a spoon, then cook for 9 minutes. Drain and rinse under cold water until completely cool. Peel and quarter. Combine the eggs with the other salad ingredients in a large bowl. Mix the dressing ingredients together using a whisk to get a thick emulsion. Pour the dressing over the salad and mix carefully so that the eggs do not break up. Serve on beds of shredded lettuce, if desired. Serves 4-6.*

*Heat the oil in a large, heavy-based saucepan and add the butter. When foaming, add the rice and cook over moderate heat for about 2 minutes, stirring constantly. When the rice begins to look opaque, add the water, salt, and pepper and bring to a boil, stirring occasionally. Cover the pan and simmer very gently, without stirring, for about 20 minutes or until all the liquid has been absorbed and the rice is tender. Stir in the herbs and green onions, cover the pan and leave to stand for about 5 minutes before serving. Serves 6.*

*Above left: the passenger sternwheeler* Natchez, *one of a number of boats to cruise the Mississippi from New Orleans. Right: Green Rice.*

# Crab Meat Imperial

Another of New Orleans' famous dishes, this makes a delicious warm weather salad for lunches, light suppers or elegant appetizers.

2 small crabs, boiled
2 Tbsps oil
4 green onions
1 small green bell pepper, finely chopped
1 stalk celery, finely chopped
1 clove garlic, minced
¾ cup prepared mayonnaise
1 Tbsp mild mustard
Dash Tabasco and Worcestershire sauce
1 piece canned pimiento, drained and finely chopped
Salt and pepper
2 Tbsps chopped parsley
Lettuce, curly endive or raddichio (optional)

To shell the crabs, first remove all the legs and the large claws by twisting and pulling them away from the body. Turn the shell over and, using your thumbs, push the body away from the flat shell. Set the body aside. Remove the stomach sack and the lungs or dead man's fingers and discard them. Using a small teaspoon, scrape the brown body meat out of the flat shell. Using a sharp knife, cut the body of the crab in four pieces and using a pick or a skewer, push out all the meat. Crack the large claws and remove the meat in one piece if possible. Crack the legs and remove the meat as well, leaving the small, thin legs in the shell. Set all the meat aside. Scrub the shells if to be used for serving. Heat the oil in a small skillet. Chop the white parts of the green onions and add to the oil with the green bell pepper, celery, and garlic. Sauté over gentle heat for about 10 minutes, stirring often to soften the vegetables but not brown them. Remove from the heat and set aside. When cool, add the mayonnaise, mustard, Tabasco, Worcestershire sauce, pimiento, some salt and pepper, and finely chopped tops of the green onions. Spoon the reserved brown body meat from the crabs back into each shell or serving dish. Gently mix the remaining crab meat with the dressing, reserving the claws for garnish, if desired, or shredding and adding to the other crab meat. Spoon into the shells on top of the brown body meat, and sprinkle with chopped parsley. Place the crab shells on serving plates, surround them with lettuce leaves and garnish with the shelled crab claws and crab legs if desired. Serves 2-4.

Right: loading bales of cotton at the busy levee.

# Shrimp Remoulade

*This classic Creole side dish, of which there are many variations, is one of New Orleans' most popular seafood salads. It can also be made with clams or scallops.*

*3 Tbsps Creole mustard or 3 Tbsps French mustard mixed with 2 tsps horseradish*
*1 Tbsp paprika*
*1 fresh chile, seeded and finely chopped*
*1 clove garlic, minced*
*Salt, to taste*
*½ cup white wine vinegar*
*1½ cups oil*
*6 green onions, sliced*
*2 stalks celery, thinly sliced*
*2 bay leaves*
*2 Tbsps chopped parsley*
*1½ pounds fresh, raw, unshelled large shrimp*
*Lettuce and lemon wedges, to serve*

*Combine the mustard, paprika, chile, garlic, and salt in a deep bowl. Mix in the vinegar thoroughly. Add the oil in a thin, steady stream while beating constantly with a small whisk. Continue to beat until the sauce is smooth and thick. Add the green onions, celery, bay leaves, and chopped parsley. Cover the bowl tightly and leave in the refrigerator for several hours, or overnight. Shell the shrimp, except for the very tail ends. If desired, the shrimp may be completely shelled. Two hours before serving, add the shrimp to the marinade and stir to coat them well. Refrigerate until ready to serve. To serve, shred the lettuce finely and place on individual serving plates. Arrange the shrimp on top and spoon over some of the marinade, discarding the bay leaves. Garnish with lemon wedges. Serves 4.*

*Above: an illustration of St. Louis Cathedral from 1886. The cathedral was extensively altered in 1851, when the famous spires were added to the towers. Facing page: traders arriving at the French market with wagonloads of goods.*

## Dirty Rice

*This dish is made with finely chopped chicken livers, and it is the appearance of the livers mixed with the rice which gives the recipe its unusual name.*

*1 cup long-grain rice*
*2 cups water*
*1 pound chicken livers, trimmed*
*1 stalk celery, roughly chopped*
*1 green bell pepper, chopped*
*2 medium onions, roughly chopped*
*2 Tbsps oil*
*Salt and pepper*
*Chopped parsley, to garnish*

*Cook the rice in the water with a pinch of salt for about 20 minutes. Leave to stand while preparing the liver. Place the livers, celery, bell pepper, and onions in a food processor and finely chop. The mixture will look soupy. Heat the oil in a large skillet and add the liver mixture. Cook over moderate heat, stirring gently. Once the mixture has set, turn down the heat to very low, cover the pan and cook about 30-40 minutes, or until rich golden brown in color. Stir in the cooked rice, fluffing up the mixture with a fork. Heat through, season to taste and serve garnished with chopped parsley. Serves 4-6.*

# CHAPTER SIX

# Cakes, Cookies and Desserts

*Above: this old view of St. Charles Avenue shows the contrasting styles of French Colonial and Greek Revival architecture.*

Baking has been a favorite pastime in the South for many generations (it has long been considered a way of showing off a cook's skill) and Cajun and Creole cooks are no exception. One of the oldest New Orleans recipes, dating back to the eighteenth century, is for Pralines. You can still see these sweet, melt-in-the-mouth cookies being made in some shops in the French Quarter. But sweet dishes are not just reserved for dessert, many – especially flambéed desserts like Bananas Foster – appear on traditional Creole brunch menus, while Beignets are eaten for breakfast with a cup New Orleans chicory-laced café au lait.

# Bread Pudding with Whiskey Sauce

*This traditional pudding can be found on the menu of any good New Orleans restaurant. It is often served with a whiskey- or brandy-laced sauce.*

## Syrup Cake

*This Cajun cake is rather like gingerbread in texture, but has the spicy taste of cinnamon, nutmeg and cloves. It can be served warm with cream or cool with coffee.*

*1 cup vegetable shortening*
*1 cup molasses*
*3 eggs*
*3 cups all-purpose flour*
*Pinch of salt*
*1 Tbsp baking powder*
*1 tsp cinnamon*
*¼ tsp ground nutmeg*
*Pinch of ground cloves*
*4 Tbsps chopped pecans*
*4 Tbsps raisins*

*Cream the shortening until light and fluffy. Add the molasses and beat with an electric mixer. Add the eggs one at a time, beating well in between each addition. Sift the flour together with the salt and baking powder. Combine with the molasses mixture and add the spices. Stir in the nuts and raisins and pour the mixture into a lightly greased 9×13 inch baking pan. Bake for about 45 minutes in a pre*

*½ loaf day-old French bread*
*2 cups milk*
*3 eggs*
*¾ cup raisins*
*1 tsp vanilla extract*
*Pinch ground ginger*
*Butter or margarine*
*½ cup butter*
*1 cup sugar*
*1 egg*
*4 Tbsps bourbon*
*Nutmeg*

*Cut the bread into small pieces and soak in the milk. When the bread has softened, add the eggs, raisins, vanilla, and ginger. Grease 8 custard cups with butter or margarine and fill each with an equal amount of pudding mixture to within ½ inch of the top. Place the dishes in a roasting pan and pour enough hot water around them to come halfway up the sides of the dishes. Bake in a preheated 350° F oven until risen and set – about 35-40 minutes. When the puddings have cooked, combine the ½ cup butter and the sugar in the top of a double boiler and heat to dissolve the sugar. Beat the egg and stir a spoonful of the hot butter mixture into it. Add the egg to the double boiler and whisk over low heat until thick. Allow to cool and add bourbon. To serve, turn out puddings onto plates and surround with sauce. Sprinkle the tops with grated nutmeg. Serves 8.*

*heated 375° F oven, or until a skewer into the center of the cake comes out clean. Allow to cool and cut into squares to serve.*
*Serves 8-12.*

*Above: the St. Charles Avenue streetcar has been operating for over a century, and is an ideal way to see the impressive plantation houses.*

# Beignets with Apricot Sauce

### Bananas Foster

This flambée recipe was originated at Brennan's, one of New Orleans' famous restaurants, and became so popular that it can now be found on any Creole menu.

4 ripe bananas, peeled
Juice of ½ lemon
½ cup butter
½ cup soft brown sugar
Pinch ground cinnamon and nutmeg
4 Tbsps orange juice
½ cup light or dark rum
Whipped cream and chopped pecans, to serve

Cut the bananas in half lengthwise and sprinkle with lemon juice on all sides. Melt the butter in a large skillet and add the sugar, spices, and orange juice. Stir over gentle heat until the sugar dissolves. Add the bananas and cook gently for about 3 minutes, without turning them, basting often. Warm the rum in a small saucepan and ignite with a match. Pour over the bananas and shake the pan gently until the flames die down. Place 2 banana halves on a serving plate and top with some cream. Sprinkle with pecans and serve immediately.
Serves 4.

These Creole doughnuts are eaten for breakfast at many of the coffee houses in the French Market.

6 Tbsps water
1 Tbsp butter or margarine
6 Tbsps all-purpose flour
3-4 eggs
Few drops vanilla extract
Oil for deep frying
Powdered sugar

APRICOT SAUCE
14 canned apricots, chopped
1 Tbsp cornstarch mixed with 4 Tbsps bourbon
Dash of lemon juice

Combine the water and butter in a pan and slowly bring to a boil. When boiling rapidly, stir in the flour quickly and remove from the heat. Beat in the eggs one at a time, beating well between each addition. Add enough so that the mixture is of dropping consistency and holds its shape well. Beat in the vanilla. Heat oil to 350° F in a deep-fat fryer or in a deep saucepan. Drop in the batter from a teaspoon and cook about four at a time, until puffed and golden. The beignets will rise to the surface when cooked and can be turned over if necessary. Drain on paper towels and dust with powdered sugar. While the beignets are cooking, combine the sauce ingredients in a heavy-based pan and bring to a boil. Cook until thickened and then transfer to a blender and purée until smooth. Serve the sauce warm with the warm beignets.
Serves 6.

Above left: after the Louisiana Purchase of 1803, when the state was bought from the French, New Orleans quickly became a world-class port. And as this 1829 engraving illustrates, the Mississippi was soon crammed with tallships and steamboats. Right: sugar being unloaded at the levee, the center of New Orleans' commercial activity.

# Crêpes à l'Orange

*Based on the French Crêpes Suzette recipe, this Creole version incorporates cream cheese and pecans.*

*1 cup all-purpose flour*
*1 Tbsp oil*
*1 whole egg, plus 1 yolk*
*1 cup milk (or more)*
*1 pound cream cheese or low fat soft cheese*
*½ cup sugar*
*Grated rind of 1 orange*
*4 Tbsps finely chopped pecans*
*Oil for frying*
*½ cup orange juice mixed with 2 tsps cornstarch*
*4 oranges, peeled and segmented*
*4 Tbsps orange liqueur*

*Sift the flour into a mixing bowl and make a well in the center. Pour the oil and egg into the well, and beat with a wooden spoon. Gradually beat in the milk, incorporating the flour slowly. Set aside for 30 minutes. Beat the cheese, sugar, and orange rind until light and fluffy. Stir in the chopped pecans and set aside. Heat a small crêpe pan or skillet and pour in a small amount of oil. Wipe over with a paper towel for a thin coating. Pour about 2 Tbsps of batter into the pan and swirl to coat the base evenly. Pour out the excess to re-use. Cook until the bottom is a light golden brown, and turn over. Cook the other side and stack up the crêpes on a plate. Repeat with remaining batter to make 12 small or 6 large crêpes. Spread some of the cream cheese filling on the speckled side of each crêpe and roll up or fold into triangles. Keep warm while preparing the sauce. Pour orange juice and cornstarch mixture into a saucepan and bring to a boil, stirring constantly until thickened and clear. Stir in the orange segments and liqueur. Spoon sauce over crêpes to serve. Serves 4-6.*

## Calas

*These small rice cakes are crisp outside, soft and light inside. Serve them hot with tea or coffee and accompany with jam.*

*1½-2 cups long-grain rice, cooked*
*1 cup all-purpose flour*
*1 tsp baking powder*
*Pinch salt*
*½ cup sugar*
*2 eggs, separated*
*6 Tbsps milk*
*Grated rind of 1 lemon*
*4 Tbsps raisins*
*Powdered sugar*
*Oil*

*Drain the cooked rice and leave to cool completely. Sift the flour, baking powder, and salt into a mixing bowl and stir in the sugar. Beat the egg yolks with the milk and add gradually to the dry ingredients, stirring constantly, to make a thick batter. Stir in the rice. Beat the egg whites until stiff but not dry, and fold into the batter with the lemon rind and raisins. Lightly oil a heavy skillet and place over moderate heat. When the pan is hot, drop in about 1 Tbsp of batter and if necessary, spread into a small circle with the back of the spoon. Cook until brown on one side and bubbles form on the top surface. Turn over and cook the other side. Cook 4-6 at a time. Repeat until all the batter is used, keeping the cakes warm. Sprinkle with powdered sugar and serve. Makes 24.*

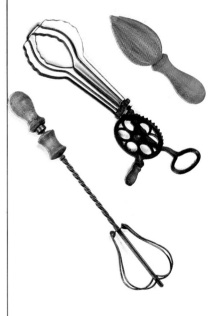

*Right: Calas.*

## Pralines

*These delicious sweet crunchy candies are a favorite in New Orleans and all over the South.*

*1½ cups unsalted butter*
*1 cup sugar*
*1 cup packed light brown sugar*
*1 cup milk*
*½ cup heavy cream*
*1 cup chopped pecans*
*2 Tbsps vanilla or rum extract*
*1 Tbsp water*
*Butter or oil*

*Melt the butter in a large, heavy-based pan. Add the sugars, milk, and cream and bring mixture to a boil, stirring constantly. Reduce the heat to simmering. Cook to a deep golden brown syrup, stirring continuously until the temperature registers 250° F ("hard ball" stage) on a candy thermometer– about 20 minutes. Add the pecans, flavoring, and water. Stir until the mixture stops foaming. Grease cookie sheets with butter or oil and drop on the mixture by spoonfuls into mounds about 2 inches in diameter. The pralines will spread out as they cool. Allow to cool completely before serving. Makes 12-16.*

# Cherries Jubilee

*This Creole dish makes a special, elegant pudding, but an easy one, too. The contrast of hot brandied cherries and cold ice cream or whipped cream is sensational.*

*1½ pounds black cherries, fresh or canned, pitted*
*2-4 Tbsps sugar*
*¾ cup brandy*
*Vanilla ice cream or whipped cream, to serve*

*If using fresh cherries, combine them with 4 Tbsps sugar in a saucepan and cook over gentle heat until the cherries soften and the juices run. If using canned cherries, combine the juice from the can with 2 Tbsps sugar and heat through to dissolve the sugar, then add the cherries. Warm the brandy in a separate saucepan, then ignite with a match. Combine the brandy with the fruit and leave until the flames die down naturally. Spoon the fruit over ice cream or serve on its own, topped with ice cream or whipped cream. Serve immediately. Serves 4-6.*

*Above: horse-drawn buggies are an ideal way to tour the French Quarter. Right: decorative ironwork balconies, or galleries, are one of the hallmarks of the beautifully preserved French Quarter.*

# Mardi Gras Cakes

*These small buns are a variation of the King's cake, made to celebrate this famous Lenten carnival in New Orleans. The three colors that are added to the icing symbolize justice, power and faith.*

1 package dried active yeast
6 Tbsps lukewarm water
2 tsps sugar
2 cups all-purpose flour
4 Tbsps additional sugar
Pinch salt
1 tsp ground ginger
Grated rind of 1 lemon
2 eggs
6 Tbsps lukewarm milk
4 Tbsps butter or margarine, cut in small pieces
4 oz mixed golden raisins, currants and chopped, candied fruit

ICING
¾ cup granulated sugar
Purple, yellow and green food colorings
2 cups powdered sugar
Juice of 1 lemon
Hot water

*Sprinkle the yeast on top of the water and stir in the sugar. Set in a warm place to prove for 15 minutes, or until bubbly. Sift the flour, sugar, salt, and ginger into a large bowl and add the lemon rind. Make a well in the center of the ingredients and pour in the yeast. Add the eggs and milk. Beat well, drawing the flour in from the outside edge, and gradually add the butter. Turn the dough out onto a well-floured surface and knead until smooth and elastic – about 10 minutes. Place the dough in a large, lightly-oiled bowl and cover with oiled plastic wrap. Leave to rise in a warm place for 1-1½ hours, or until doubled in bulk. Punch down the dough and knead in the fruit to distribute it evenly. Oil a 12-space muffin pan. Divide the dough into 12 and knead each piece into a smooth ball. Place a ball in each space in the pan and cover lightly. Leave in a warm place for 20-30 minutes to rise a second time. Bake at 375° F for about 20-25 minutes, or until golden brown. Allow to cool slightly and loosen the cakes. Cool completely before removing from the pan. Place an equal portion of granulated sugar in each of three jars and add a drop of different food coloring to each. Shake the jars to color the sugar. Sift the powdered sugar into a bowl and mix with the lemon juice. Add enough hot water to make an icing that pours easily but still coats the back of a spoon. Spoon some icing over each cake and sprinkle the cakes with the different colored sugars before the icing sets.*
*Makes 12.*

## Brown Sugar Cookies

*These cookies can also be made with raisins. The thick dough bakes to a crisp, golden brown cookie, which is perfect as an accompaniment to ice-cream or fruit salad.*

*1¼ cups packed light brown sugar*
*3 Tbsps light corn syrup*
*4 Tbsps water*
*1 egg*
*2⅓ cups all-purpose flour*
*1 Tbsp ground ginger*
*1 Tbsp baking soda*
*Pinch salt*
*1 cup finely chopped pecans*

*Mix the brown sugar, syrup, water and egg together in a large bowl. Beat with an electric mixer until pale. Sift flour, ginger, baking soda, and salt into the brown sugar mixture and add the pecans. Stir by hand until thoroughly mixed. Lightly oil three cookie sheets and drop the mixture on by spoonfuls, about 2 inches apart. Bake in a pre-heated 375° F oven until lightly browned around the edges – about 10-12 minutes. Leave on the cookie sheet for 1-2 minutes before removing with a spatula to a wire rack to cool completely. Makes about 36.*

# Oreilles de Cochon

*These light, delicate pastries have a rather unusual name – Pig's Ears! It refers strictly to the shape the dough takes when deep-fried.*

*1 cup all-purpose flour*
*1 tsp baking powder*
*¼ tsp salt*
*4 Tbsps cold water*
*Oil for deep frying*
*1½ cups cane syrup mixed with ¾ cup molasses*
*3 oz finely chopped pecans*

*Sift the flour, baking powder, and salt together in a large bowl. Make a well in the center and pour in the cold water. Using a wooden spoon, mix until a stiff dough forms, and then knead by hand until smooth. Divide the dough into 12 portions, each about the size of a walnut. Roll out each portion on a floured surface until very thin. Heat the oil in a deep-fat fryer to 350° F. Drop in each piece of pastry using two forks. Twist the pastry just as it hits the oil. Cook one at a time until light brown. In a large saucepan, boil the syrup until it forms a soft ball when dropped into cold water, or 240° F on a candy thermometer. Drain the pastries on paper towels and dip carefully into the hot syrup. Sprinkle with pecans before the syrup sets and allow to cool before serving. Makes 12.*

*Above left: a wood engraving from 1861 depicting confederate troops with stolen U.S. wagons. Below: Soniat House on Chartres Street, built about 1829, has a lovely cast-iron lacework gallery.*

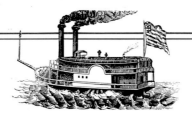

# Index

## ACKNOWLEDGEMENTS

The publishers would like to thank the following organizations
and individuals for contributing to this book: Archive Photos;
American Stock; Zeva Olebaum; Sue Philpot; Louisa Verney.